1O Facts About...

10
Facts
About...

Aaron Erhardt

EP

ERHARDT PUBLICATIONS

LOUISVILLE, KENTUCKY

2013

Dedication

Judy Bussey & Stephen Sebree
"fellow workers" for the truth
(3 John 8)

Table of Contents

Abortion

(1) Elizabeth conceived a "son"

(2) Unborn child is called a "life"

(3) Unborn child is called a "baby"

(4) To be pregnant is to be "with child"

(5) God hears the cries of innocent blood

(6) God hates hands that shed innocent blood

(7) God has a special relationship with the unborn

(8) God blessed those who protected unborn children

(9) Personhood is never measured by age/development

(10) Early church writers strongly condemned abortion

Footnotes

(1) Luke 1:36.
(2) Exodus 21:22-25.
(3) Luke 1:41-44.
(4) Matthew 1:18; Genesis 25:22.
(5) Genesis 4:10.
(6) Proverbs 6:16-17.
(7) Psalm 139:13-16; Jeremiah 1:5.
(8) Exodus 1:15-21.
(10) Clement, Tertullian, Jerome, etc.

Abortion was pushed to the forefront of American politics when the United States Supreme Court ruled on the infamous *Roe v. Wade* case in 1973. The Court voted 7-2 to strike down Texas abortion laws and deemed abortion to be a fundamental right up to the point of viability. *Doe v. Bolton* was a lesser-known case decided at the same time. Abortion was legalized in every state.

For those of us who believe that human life begins at conception, abortion is much more than a political issue. It is a moral issue. It is a Gospel issue. If life begins at conception, then any deliberate act to end a pregnancy is murder. Abortion becomes an act of violence that takes the life of an innocent child.

The Arguments

(1) *A woman has a right to control her own body.* While it is true that a woman should control her own body, the baby's body is not her own. It is a different body with a genetic code that differs from the mother's. A woman's body does not have two hearts, heads, and blood types.

(2) *We cannot know if the fetus is a human being.* If that is so, shouldn't the benefit of the doubt go to preserving life? Scripture teaches and science affirms that the unborn are living human beings.

> If you don't know whether a body is alive or dead, you would never bury it. I think this consideration itself should be enough for all of us to insist on protecting the unborn (Ronald Reagan, Abortion and the Conscience of the Nation article).

(3) *It is better to abort a child than abuse one.* Abortion is the worst form of child abuse. What could be more abusive than cutting someone into pieces or burning them to death with poison?

(4) *We cannot impose our morality on others.* Wouldn't this same argument apply to murder or rape? Those who make this argument are the very people trying to impose their *immorality* on others!

(5) *People are going to have abortions anyway.* Again, this same argument could apply to murder or rape. Because people are going to murder anyway, should we go ahead and legalize murder? Laws do affect behavior and change attitudes.

(6) *Rape victims should be able to abort the child.* The violence of abortion parallels the violence of rape. Why should the innocent child suffer the death penalty for the actions of his father? Abortion will not bring healing to the woman, it will only add to the shame. (Let it be noted that less than 1% of abortions are performed as a result of rape).

(7) *If we outlaw abortions, many women will die in back alleys.* The number of mothers who may die in back alleys trying to have an abortion pales in comparison to the number of babies dying each day in abortion clinics.

There are other arguments, but these are the most common ones. There is no good reason to kill an innocent child. Abortion cannot be justified!

The Bible

When Mary went to visit her pregnant relative Elizabeth, we read that the "baby" leaped in Elizabeth's womb (Luke 1:41, 44). That is the same word *(brephos)* used in the next chapter to describe a child after birth (Luke 2:12). Hence, God views those in the womb and those out of the womb the same — both are babies!

Personhood was never measured by age or stage of development in scripture. From the moment of conception in the depths of the womb one was recognized as a human being created in the image of God. That is why to be pregnant was to be "with child" (Matthew 1:18) and the angel Gabriel told Mary that her relative Elizabeth conceived "a son" (Luke 1:36).

There are many passages that indicate God has a special relationship with the unborn (Job 10:8-12; Psalm 139:13-16; Jeremiah 1:4-5). There is a pre-birth relationship that exists between the Creator and His creation.

Some argue that abortion is not murder because the fetus has not yet received the "breath of life" spoken of in Genesis 2:7. However, that passage speaks specifically about Adam, one who sprang into existence fully grown having been formed from the dust of the ground. That was a unique situation. The rest of us receive the "breath of life" long before we begin to breathe independently of our mothers. We breathe (i.e., receive oxygen) through our mothers while in the womb.

No conception ever occurs that is not the result of God's creative purposes (Genesis 17:16; 21:2; Ruth 4:13). Therefore, we must not tamper with what God has done. His Word teaches that life begins at conception long before the body is formed. Abortion robs God of His glory and the child of his life!

Angels

(1) "Angel" means "messenger"

(2) Angels were created by God

(3) Angels who sin are punished

(4) Angels do not experience death

(5) Angels do not marry one another

(6) Angels are said to be innumerable

(7) Angels do not bring new revelation

(8) Angels will be at the Second Coming

(9) Angels are not to be objects of worship

(10) Gabriel and Michael are angels of God

Footnotes

(1) The word is used of both human and heavenly messengers in NT.

(2) Psalm 148:2-5.

(3) 2 Peter 2:4; Jude 6; Matthew 25:41.

(4) Luke 20:36.

(5) Mark 12:25.

(6) Hebrews 12:22.

(7) Galatians 1:6-9.

(8) Matthew 16:27; 25:31; 2 Thessalonians 1:7.

(9) Colossians 2:18; Revelation 19:10; 22:9.

(10) Luke 1:19; Jude 9.

Baptism

(1) Baptism is immersion

(2) Baptism is a command

(3) Baptism is for salvation

(4) Baptism is for believers

(5) Baptism is for forgiveness

(6) Baptism is an urgent matter

(7) Baptism puts one into Christ

(8) Baptism is not for a Christian

(9) Baptism occurs before rejoicing

(10) Preaching Jesus includes baptism

Footnotes

(1) Romans 6:3-5; Colossians 2:12-13.

(2) Acts 10:48.

(3) Mark 16:16; 1 Peter 3:21.

(4) Mark 16:16; Acts 8:12-13, 36-37 (KJV).

(5) Acts 2:38; 22:16.

(6) Acts 22:16.

(7) Romans 6:3; Galatians 3:27.

(8) Baptism is to become a Christian.

(9) Acts 8:39; 16:34.

(10) Acts 8:12, 35-36.

The Bible

(1) It is inspired

(2) It is infallible

(3) It is complete

(4) It is understandable

(5) It is a library of 66 books

(6) It was written in three languages

(7) It was written by about 40 writers

(8) It was divided into chapters in 1250

(9) It has been providentially preserved

(10) It will be the standard of judgment

Footnotes
(1) 2 Timothy 3:16; 2 Peter 1:21; 2 Samuel 23:2.
(2) John 10:35.
(3) John 16:13; 2 Peter 1:3; Jude 3.
(4) John 8:32; Ephesians 3:4; 5:17; 1 Timothy 2:4.
(6) Hebrew and Greek with scattered Aramaic.
(9) 1 Peter 1:23-25.
(10) John 12:48; Romans 2:16.

The Bible has had an enormous impact on the world. It has influenced cultures and shaped nations. It has been copied and circulated more extensively than any other literature, and has been translated into about two thousand languages. But is the Bible from God?

Is The Bible From God?

(1) Unity
The Bible is a library of 66 books. There are 39 books in the Old Testament and 27 books in the New Testament. It was written over a span of about sixteen hundred years (1500 B.C. — 100 A.D.) by more than forty writers. The writers were not always aware of one another's writings and sometimes did not even know the meaning of their own words (1 Peter 1:10-12). Yet the Bible fits together perfectly. There are no contradictions or inconsistencies.

The writers could hardly have come from more diverse backgrounds. They were shepherds, statesmen, prophets, priests, kings, physicians, fishermen, and tax collectors. They were wealthy and poor, educated and uneducated. They wrote from palaces and prisons, in times of peace and times of war. Furthermore, the Bible was written in three different languages on three different continents. There is no way that mere men from such diverse backgrounds could have written the Bible in such a unified manner without divine guidance. The unity of the Bible proves that it is from God!

(2) Accuracy
Although the Bible was not written as a textbook on geography, history, or science, it is always accurate in those areas. One of the most fascinating studies of the Bible's accuracy is in the field of archaeology. For instance, Genesis 40 mentions grapes in Egypt. Yet some had contended that the Egyptians never grew grapes or drank wine. However, archaeology has proven that there were grapes in Egypt. Tombs have been discovered which depict the dressing and pruning of vines, and scenes of drunkenness. Another example is the Hittite nation. For a long time critics denied that the Hittites ever existed. However, excavations in Turkey have uncovered their existence.

The ancient Egyptians were renowned for their medical advancements. However, we now know that some of their practices were actually harmful to the patient. For instance, the famous Ebers Papyrus, a medical document of the Egyptians (1552 B.C.), indicates that they would prescribe animal dung for patients. This is significant because Moses was "instructed in all the wisdom of the Egyptians" (Acts 7:22), yet he never included any of their harmful practices in his writings. What are the chances that a man educated in the ways of the Egyptians would not incorporate at least some of the faulty remedies of the Egyptians in his writings? Not only that, but every instruction given by Moses has been proven correct by modern medicine. Circumcision on the eighth day, the quarantine of lepers, burning contaminated clothing, burying waste, forbidding the eating of blood, etc. are all proper instructions.

The Bible told us that God "hangs the earth on nothing" (Job 26:7) and "sits above the circle of the earth" (Isaiah 40:22) before we knew that the earth hangs from nothing and is round.

(3) Fairness
In most books, there are heroes and villains. The heroes are presented favorably and flawlessly. However, such is not the case with the Bible. It makes no attempts to hide the mistakes of its heroes. For instance, Noah's drunkenness (Genesis 9), Abraham's lies (Genesis 12, 20), Moses' presumption (Numbers 20), David's adultery (2 Samuel 11), and Peter's denials (Matthew 26) are all plainly revealed. There is no attempt to excuse or shield their shortcomings. Human authors only present the good side of their heroes. God presents the good, the bad, and the ugly!

(4) Prophecy
The Bible is a book of prophecy. Many of these prophecies were uttered hundreds of years before their fulfillment. For instance, it was prophesied that the Messiah would be born of the virgin (Isaiah 7:14) in the town of Bethlehem (Micah 5:2). It was also prophesied that He would be preceded by a messenger (Isaiah 40:3), betrayed for thirty pieces of silver (Zechariah 11:12-13), pierced in the hands and feet (Psalm 22:16), numbered with the transgressors (Isaiah 53:12), buried in a rich man's tomb (Isaiah 53:9), and resurrected from the dead (Psalm 16:10). All of these prophecies, and countless others, came to pass! Could men ut-

ter predications hundreds of years before their fulfillment with such stunning detail without making a mistake? The very thought is absurd. Yet Bible prophecies did just that!

(5) Preservation

The Bible has been the object of much persecution. On many occasions men have sought to ban and destroy it, but their efforts have always failed. Others have scrutinized the Bible trying to find contradictions that would prove it false, but to no avail. The Bible has survived the scrutiny. The fact that the Bible continues to exist intact and to possess the same strengths today that it has always possessed proves that it is from God.

There is more evidence that proves the Bible is from God. However, these points are more than sufficient. The writers claimed to be inspired (2 Samuel 23:2; 1 Corinthians 14:37; 1 Thessalonians 2:13) and the evidence proves that their claims were true. No other book can do what the Bible does. No other book can pass the tests the Bible passes. The Bible is from God (2 Timothy 3:16)!

Calvinism

(1) Calvinism is named after John Calvin

(2) Calvin was a leader of the Reformation

(3) Calvin was strongly influenced by Augustine

(4) Calvinism is a system of religious beliefs

(5) Calvinism has five major tenets (TULIP)

(6) Total Hereditary Depravity is the first tenet

(7) Unconditional Election is the second tenet

(8) Limited Atonement is the third tenet

(9) Irresistible Grace is the fourth tenet

(10) Perseverance of the Saints is the fifth tenet

Footnotes

(1) John Calvin was born on July 10, 1509 (France) and died on May 27, 1564 (Switzerland).

(2) The Reformation was a sixteenth century religious movement.

(3) Augustine of Hippo (354-430 A.D.) framed many of Calvin's doctrines.

(5) TULIP is the acronym by which Calvinism is summed up.

(6) Man is born in sin with a corrupt nature and unable to do any good.

(7) God arbitrarily chose a fixed number to be saved before the world began.

(8) Christ died only for the elect.

(9) The Holy Spirit miraculously draws the elect to Christ.

(10) It is impossible for the elect to fall away.

ohn Calvin (1509-1564) was born in France to Roman Catholic parents. He left Roman Catholicism around 1530 and later fled to Switzerland where he published *Institutes of the Christian Religion.* Calvin, who was heavily influenced by the writings of Augustine, became the prominent figure in the development of a system of beliefs later called Calvinism.

The five major tenets of Calvinism are summed up by the acronym TULIP: Total Hereditary Depravity; Unconditional Election; Limited Atonement; Irresistible Grace; and Perseverance of the Saints. The five tenets are mutually dependent and logically connected. They are all false!

Total Hereditary Depravity is the belief that man is born in sin with a corrupt nature and unable to do any good. However, the Bible says "God made man upright" (Ecclesiastes 7:29), "the son shall not suffer for the iniquity of the father" (Ezekiel 18:20), and "all we like sheep *have gone* astray" (Isaiah 53:6, emp. mine). Furthermore, Paul spoke of some who "by nature" did good (Romans 2:14), and recalled a time in his life when he was "alive" spiritually apart from the law (Romans 7:9).

Paul told the Corinthians to be "infants in evil" (1 Corinthians 14:20). He would have never said that if he believed that infants were born in sin with a corrupt nature and unable to do any good. The expression "infants in evil" in 1 Corinthians 14:20 parallels the expression "innocent in evil" in Romans 16:19. Hence, infants are innocent!

Unconditional Election is the belief that God arbitrarily chose a certain number of people to be saved before the foundation of the world. However, the Bible says "God shows no partiality" (Romans 2:11), "desires all people to be saved" (1 Timothy 2:4), and is "not wishing that any should perish, but that all should reach repentance" (2 Peter 3:9). God predestined that those in Christ would be saved (Ephesians 1:4). He did not predestine who would be in Christ.

Limited Atonement is the belief that Christ died only for the elect. However, the Bible says Christ "has died for all" (2 Corinthians 5:14), tasted death "for everyone" (Hebrews 2:9), and is the propitiation "for the sins of the whole world" (1 John 2:2).

Irresistible Grace is the belief that the Holy Spirit miraculously draws the elect to Christ regardless of their desire. However, the Bible says the gospel "is the power of God for salvation" (Romans 1:16) and that we are converted "through the gospel" (1 Corinthians 4:15). The Holy Spirit draws man to Christ though the preached Word, not separate and apart from it. Furthermore, man has a free will. He can "resist the Holy Spirit" (Acts 7:51) and "quench the Spirit" (1 Thessalonians 5:19).

Perseverance of the Saints is the belief that it is impossible for the elect to fall away and be lost. However, the Bible says that we can "fall" (1 Corinthians 10:12), "fall away from the living God" (Hebrews 3:12), and "fall by the same sort of disobedience" (Hebrews 4:11). Paul knew that he could be "disqualified" (1 Corinthians 9:27), and spoke of some who would "depart from the faith" (1 Timothy 4:1). Likewise, Peter spoke of those who would "turn back from the holy commandment" (2 Peter 2:21). We even have actual examples of people who fell away: Ananias and Sapphira (Acts 5:1-11), Hymenaeus and Alexander (1 Timothy 1:20), Demas (2 Timothy 4:10), and Diotrephes (3 John 9-10). Salvation is conditioned upon man's continued obedience. He can fall away!

Calvinism asserts that man is wholly passive in redemption. There is nothing he can do. He is reduced to a robot with no free moral agency. Furthermore, God is made the ultimate respecter of persons, divine favor becomes divine force, preaching is unnecessary, and scripture is insufficient. Who can believe such a thing?

Calvinism has had a tremendous impact on the religious world. Many denominations accept one or more parts of the aforementioned TULIP. Therefore, we must teach others that Calvinism is erroneous.

Capital Punishment

(1) Capital punishment is not murder

(2) It was authorized in the New Law

(3) It was incorporated in the Old Law

(4) It is rooted in respect for human life

(5) Some crimes merit the death penalty

(6) The government is to punish evildoers

(7) Punishment should be carried out quickly

(8) The authority to execute comes from above

(9) Failing to execute murderers pollutes the land

(10) Private retaliation is condemned in New Law

Footnotes

(1) Murder is "unlawful" killing.
(2) Acts 25:11; Romans 13:1-4.
(3) Numbers 35:16-21.
(4) Genesis 9:6.
(5) Acts 25:11.
(6) 1 Peter 2:13-15.
(7) Ecclesiastes 8:11.
(8) John 19:10-11.
(9) Numbers 35:31-34.
(10) Matthew 5:38-39; Romans 12:19.

Christians

(1) "Christians" follow Christ

(2) The name appears three times

(3) The name was divinely revealed

(4) The name was not given in derision

(5) The name was first given in Antioch

(6) The name was not worn with a hyphen

(7) Christians are servants, saints, and priests

(8) Christians are those belonging to the Way

(9) Christians are those who obeyed the gospel

(10) "Christian" is not the new name of Isaiah 62:2

Footnotes

(2) Acts 11:26; 26:28; 1 Peter 4:16.

(3) "Called" is used of a divine calling in NT.

(4) There is nothing offensive in the name.

(5) Acts 11:26.

(6) Baptist-Christians, Methodist-Christians, etc.

(7) 2 Timothy 2:24; Philippians 1:1; 1 Peter 2:5, 9.

(8) Acts 9:2; 19:9, 23; 22:4; 24:14, 22.

(9) Galatians 5:7; 1 Peter 4:16-17.

(10) Isaiah says the name was "Hephzibah" (62:4).

Christmas

(1) Jesus was born in Bethlehem

(2) When Jesus was born is unknown

(3) Jesus never commanded Christmas

(4) The apostles never observed Christmas

(5) We are to commemorate the Lord's death

(6) We are not to observe unauthorized holy days

(7) December 25th was originally a pagan observance

(8) "Christmas" is of Catholic origin (Mass of Christ)

(9) The unknown number of wise men went to the house

(10) It is not wrong to observe Christmas as a civil holiday

Footnotes

(1) Matthew 2:1; Luke 2:6; Micah 5:2.

(2) Shepherds were in the fields from April-October (Luke 2:8).

(4) Christmas was not observed until the fourth century.

(5) Matthew 26:26-29; 1 Corinthians 11:23-26.

(6) Galatians 4:10.

(7) It was celebrated among the Romans in honor of the sun-god.

(9) Matthew 2:11.

(10) This falls into same category as circumcising for reasons non-religious.

The church of Christ

(1) "Church" means "assembly"

(2) The term is used in two senses

(3) The saved are added to the church

(4) The church was eternally purposed

(5) The church was promised by the Lord

(6) The church was established in Jerusalem

(7) The church wears the name of its founder

(8) The church is not the literal meeting house

(9) The church is the body, bride, and kingdom

(10) Man-made denominations rival the church

Footnotes
(1) Acts 19:32, 39, 41. (Etymology: "called out").
(2) The two senses are universal and local.
(3) Ephesians 5:23; Acts 2:47, KJV.
(4) Ephesians 3:10-11.
(5) Matthew 16:18.
(6) Acts 2:1-47; Isaiah 2:2-4; Micah 4:1-2.
(7) Romans 16:16.
(9) Colossians 1:18; Ephesians 5:23; Colossians 1:13.

Church Organization

(1) Early churches were autonomous

(2) Elders and deacons were appointed

(3) Elders were overseers of the church

(4) Deacons were servants of the church

(5) Members were to submit to the elders

(6) Preachers had a set work in the church

(7) The elders have no legislative authority

(8) The elders must meet divine qualifications

(9) Every church is to have a plurality of elders

(10) Human oversight from without is unscriptural

Footnotes

(1) Each congregation was self-governing.

(2) Philippians 1:1; 1 Timothy 3:1-13.

(3) Acts 20:28; 1 Peter 5:2.

(4) Acts 6:1-6.

(5) Hebrews 13:17; 1 Thessalonians 5:12.

(6) 2 Timothy 4:5.

(7) James 4:12.

(8) 1 Timothy 3:1-7; Titus 1:5-9.

(9) Acts 14:23; 15:4; 20:17; Philippians 1:1; James 5:14.

(10) No outside boards, councils, general assemblies, etc.

Creation

(1) The universe was created by God

(2) The universe was created "ex nihilo"

(3) The universe was spoken into existence

(4) Creation is a completed event of the past

(5) The six days of creation were literal days

(6) The universe was created in a mature state

(7) The first man was created around 4004 B.C.

(8) The universe will be destroyed on the last day

(9) "Mother Nature" is rooted in pagan mythology

(10) Man and dinosaur lived on earth at the same time

Footnotes

(1) Genesis 1:1.

(2) Hebrews 11:3. This denies the pre-existence of matter.

(3) Genesis 1:3-31; Psalm 33:6-9.

(4) Acts 14:15; Colossians 1:16; Hebrews 1:2.

(5) The days correspond to the days of Israelite labor (Exodus 20:9-11).

(6) Trees bore fruit (Genesis 1:12), man could procreate (Genesis 1:28), etc.

(8) 2 Peter 3:10-12; Matthew 24:25.

(10) Both were created on day six (Genesis 1:24-27).

Demon Possession

(1) Demons are evil spirits

(2) Demons are agents of Satan

(3) Demon possession was temporary

(4) Demon possession ceased with miracles

(5) Demon possession is not occurring today

(6) Demon possession resulted in many ailments

(7) Demon possession was distinct from diseases

(8) Demon possession demonstrated Jesus' power

(9) Demon possession was not part of Old Testament

(10) Demon possession affected men, women, and children

Footnotes

(1) Matthew 8:16; Luke 6:18; 7:21.

(2) Matthew 12:24.

(3) It flourished at the time of Christ and then gradually diminished.

(4) It ceased when the corresponding gift of expulsion ceased.

(7) Matthew 4:24; 8:16.

(8) Mark 1:27.

(9) Saul is the only possible exception (1 Samuel 16:14).

(10) Matthew 9:32; Luke 8:2; Mark 7:30.

Dinosaurs

(1) "Dinosaur" means "terribly great lizard"

(2) The term "dinosaur" was coined in 1842

(3) Dinosaurs were actual creatures on earth

(4) Dinosaurs and humans coexisted on earth

(5) Dinosaurs went extinct after the great flood

(6) "Behemoth" may have been a land-dinosaur

(7) "Leviathan" may have been a water-dinosaur

(8) Indian carvings depict a plant-eating dinosaur

(9) All land-living animals were created on day 6

(10) Earth was created less than 10,000 years ago

Footnotes
(2) It was coined by a British anatomist named Sir Richard Owen.
(4) All land-living animals were created on the same day as mankind.
(6) Job 40:15-18. ESV footnote: "A large animal, exact identity unknown."
(7) Job 41:1-34. ESV footnote: "A large sea animal, exact identity unknown."
(8) Indian carvings are at Kachina Bridge in Utah and predate A.D.1500.
(9) Genesis 1:24-31.

What does the Bible say about dinosaurs? Were they real creatures? If so, when did they go extinct? Do dinosaurs disprove the Genesis account of creation? Do dinosaurs help the evolutionists? These are good questions that deserve an answer.

In 1822, a man named Gideon Mantell discovered an unusual fossil of animal teeth. Unable to identify the large animal from which the teeth came, he referred to it as "iguanodon," meaning iguana tooth. By 1842, so many fossils had been discovered that a British anatomist named Sir Richard Owen coined the term "dinosaur," meaning terribly great lizard.

Evolutionists teach that dinosaurs lived on the earth millions of years before humans, and that no human has ever seen a live dinosaur. However, there is overwhelming evidence that the evolutionists are wrong. Dinosaurs and humans coexisted on the earth. For instance, in the early 1940s, clay figurines were discovered in Mexico. The figurines, which were determined to be 4,500 years old, were of different animals, including an animal which strongly resembled dinosaurs. That is significant because it places humans on earth with dinosaurs. The only way they could have accurately depicted dinosaurs is if they saw them!

"The Natural Bridges National Monument" is located in a desolate area of southeastern Utah. There are three natural bridges there: Sipapu Bridge, Kachina Bridge, and Owachomo Bridge. At the bottom of the Kachina Bridge, there are Indian petroglyphs which predate A.D. 1500. One of the petroglyphs is of a plant-eating dinosaur. Again, the only way they could have accurately depicted dinosaurs is if they saw them! It should also be noted that "The Dinosaur Museum" is not far from the natural bridges and contains hip-bone fragments of a plant-eating dinosaur.

The Bible teaches that all land-living animals, including dinosaurs, were created on day 6 of creation. That is the same day that man was created. Hence, humans and dinosaurs coexisted on the earth.

Some have questioned why the Bible does not mention dinosaurs. First, there are many animals that are not mentioned in the Bible. Second, the term "dinosaur" was not coined until 1842. That was long after the King

James Version of 1611! Third, I do believe that the Bible speaks of dinosaurs, although they are not called by that name. In Job 40:15-18 we read about "Behemoth."

> Behold, Behemoth, which I made as I made you; he eats grass like an ox. Behold, his strength in his loins, and his power in the muscles of his belly. He makes his tail stiff like a cedar; the sinews of his thighs are knit together. His bones are tubes of bronze, his limbs like bars of iron.

What is "Behemoth?" The ESV footnote says at this place: "A large animal, exact identity unknown." While some suggest that the animal described is an elephant or hippo, the context seems to prove otherwise. For instance, Behemoth "eats grass like an ox" (v. 15). That rules out an elephant. Behemoth also "makes his tail stiff like a cedar" (v. 17). That rules out a hippo. This writer believes that Behemoth is what we know as a dinosaur!

Some have questioned how Noah could have fit dinosaurs on the ark. Since the evidence mentioned above does indicate that dinosaurs existed after the flood, Noah must have carried some on the ark. However, that does not mean he took full-grown dinosaurs on the ark. Perhaps he took the smaller dinosaurs. Not all dinosaurs were huge; some were roughly the size of dogs.

Although we cannot answer all the questions about dinosaurs, we do know that they were created on day 6 of creation. Some of the dinosaurs survived the flood, but like other animals eventually went extinct. Evolutionists have no friend in the dinosaur!

Divine Providence

(1) "Providence" means "foresight"

(2) Providence does not violate natural law

(3) Providence does not violate human will

(4) Providence is taught throughout the Bible

(5) Providence is not to be confused with miracles

(6) Prayer depends on a belief in divine providence

(7) God works providentially in the affairs of people

(8) God works providentially in the affairs of nations

(9) The story of Joseph is a great example of providence

(10) A proper understanding of providence relieves worry

Footnotes

(1) Acts 24:2, KJV.

(4) Genesis 45:4-8; 50:20; Ruth 2:3; Esther 4:14; Philemon 15; etc.

(5) Providence is God working within natural law and circumstance.

(6) Matthew 24:20; Colossians 4:3; 1 Timothy 2:1-2.

(7) Joseph, Ruth, Esther, Onesimus, etc.

(8) The rise and preservation of the Israelite nation.

(9) The empty pit, slave-traders headed for Egypt, cupbearer encounter, etc.

(10) Matthew 6:26-34.

Easter

(1) Jesus was raised from the dead

(2) Jesus never commanded Easter

(3) The apostles never observed Easter

(4) The resurrection is bedrock of faith

(5) The resurrection is commemorated

(6) The term "Easter" is a mistranslation

(7) We must reject unauthorized holy days

(8) Easter is a moveable holiday on calendar

(9) Easter is an unauthorized human tradition

(10) Easter can be observed as a civil holiday

Footnotes
(1) Matthew 28:1-8; 1 Corinthians 15:3-5.
(3) Easter was not observed until the second century.
(4) 1 Corinthians 15:12-19; Romans 1:4; 1 Peter 1:3.
(5) It is commemorated by our first day of the week assembly.
(6) Acts 12:4, KJV. The word (*pascha*) should be translated "Passover."
(7) Galatians 4:10.
(8) It falls on a Sunday between March 22 and April 25.
(9) Mark 7:8; Colossians 2:8.
(10) It falls into same category as circumcising for reasons non-religious.

Elders

(1) "Elder" is used in two senses

(2) Elders must meet qualifications

(3) Elders are to be in every church

(4) Elders are to care for the church

(5) Elders are to watch for our souls

(6) Elders are to be examples for all

(7) Elders are not to be domineering

(8) Elders are to be obeyed by the flock

(9) Members are to esteem the elders

(10) The oversight of elders is limited

Footnotes

(1) It is used in general sense (older person) and in specific sense (overseer).

(2) 1 Timothy 3:1-7; Titus 1:5-9.

(3) Acts 14:23; 15:4; 20:17; Philippians 1:1; James 5:14.

(4) Acts 20:28; 1 Timothy 3:5.

(5) Hebrews 13:17.

(6) 1 Peter 5:3.

(7) 1 Peter 5:3. Elders should not act like Diotrephes (3 John 9-10).

(8) Hebrews 13:17.

(9) 1 Thessalonians 5:12-13.

(10) Acts 20:28; 1 Peter 5:2.

Fasting

(1) "Fasting" is to abstain from food

(2) Fasting is not for self-promotion

(3) Fasting was common among the Jews

(4) One fast was commanded in the Old Law

(5) Jesus and the disciples fasted on occasion

(6) The Pharisees fasted two times each week

(7) Fasting is not commanded in the New Law

(8) Fasting can be a legitimate form of devotion

(9) Fasting was inserted into some texts by scribes

(10) Fasting is behind the name of the morning meal

Footnotes
(1) It is an act of self-denial wherein one abstains from food.
(2) Matthew 6:16-18.
(3) Moses, David, Elijah, Nehemiah, etc. are notable examples.
(5) Matthew 4:2; Acts 13:3; 14:23.
(6) Luke 18:12 (second and fifth days).
(7) There is no mention of time, place, method, etc.
(9) Matthew 17:21; Mark 9:29; Acts 10:30; 1 Corinthians 7:5.
(10) "Breakfast" is so named because one "breaks fast" from night before.

Final Judgment

(1) Judgment will come

(2) People will be judged

(3) Angels will be judged

(4) Jesus will be the Judge

(5) Our deeds will be known

(6) The saved will be rewarded

(7) The wicked will be punished

(8) The Word will be the standard

(9) It will follow the Lord's return

(10) Saints will participate with Jesus

Footnotes

(1) Matthew 25:31-46; Acts 17:31; 24:25.
(2) 2 Corinthians 5:10; Hebrews 9:27.
(3) 2 Peter 2:4; Jude 6.
(4) John 5:22; Acts 10:42; 2 Timothy 4:1, 8.
(5) 2 Corinthians 5:10.
(6) Matthew 25:34-40.
(7) Matthew 25:41-46.
(8) John 12:48; Romans 2:16.
(9) Matthew 25:31-32.
(10) 1 Corinthians 6:2-3.

The Holy Spirit

(1) There are three persons of Deity

(2) The Holy Spirit is a divine person

(3) The Holy Spirit was active in creation

(4) The Holy Spirit was active in revelation

(5) The Holy Spirit was active in redemption

(6) The Holy Spirit works through the gospel

(7) The Holy Spirit dwells in children of God

(8) The Holy Spirit gave spiritual gifts to men

(9) The Holy Spirit can be resisted and outraged

(10) The Holy Spirit's activities are misrepresented

Footnotes

(1) Matthew 3:16-17; 28:19; Acts 10:38; 2 Corinthians 13:14.

(2) Acts 5:3-4. He hears, speaks, leads, loves, comforts, etc.

(3) Genesis 1:2.

(4) 2 Peter 1:21.

(5) Hebrews 9:14.

(6) Ephesians 6:17.

(7) Romans 8:9-11; 1 Corinthians 3:16; 2 Timothy 1:14.

(8) 1 Corinthians 12:4-11.

(9) Acts 7:51; Hebrews 10:29.

(10) Some say chaotic, disorderly behavior is Spirit-driven (1 Corinthians 14:40).

Holy Spirit Baptism

(1) There are six baptisms in NT

(2) Holy Spirit baptism was predicted by John

(3) Holy Spirit baptism was performed by Jesus

(4) The apostles were baptized in the Holy Spirit

(5) Cornelius' house was baptized in the Holy Spirit

(6) Holy Spirit baptism was not a common occurrence

(7) Holy Spirit baptism was a promise, not a command

(8) Holy Spirit baptism was never urged on other people

(9) Holy Spirit baptism had ceased by writing of Ephesians

(10) The benefits of Holy Spirit baptism extend to us today

Footnotes

(1) Holy Spirit, fire, suffering, Great Commission, John, and Moses.

(2) Matthew 3:11.

(3) Luke 3:16.

(4) Acts 2:4; 11:15. This was for inspiration and confirmation.

(5) Acts 10:44; 11:15. This was to bear witness that Gentiles could be saved (15:8).

(6) There are only two recorded occurrences (Acts 2; 10).

(9) Ephesians 4:5. The "one baptism" was in water (1 Peter 3:21).

(10) We benefit from the inspiration of the apostles and the inclusion of the Gentiles.

The Home

(1) The home is God-ordained

(2) The home consists of people

(3) Husbands are to be the leaders

(4) Husbands are to be the providers

(5) Husbands are to love their wives

(6) Wives are to respect their husbands

(7) Wives are to be submissive homemakers

(8) Children are to be taught the ways of God

(9) Children are to be obedient to their parents

(10) The home as God described is under attack

Footnotes

(1) There are three God-ordained institutions (home, church, and government).

(2) The first home had a husband, a wife, and children.

(3) Ephesians 5:23; 1 Corinthians 11:3.

(4) 1 Timothy 5:8.

(5) Ephesians 5:25-33.

(6) Ephesians 5:33.

(7) Titus 2:5; 1 Timothy 5:14.

(8) Ephesians 6:4; Deuteronomy 6:4-9

(9) Ephesians 6:1; Romans 1:30.

(10) Gay marriage, singles adopting, raising children without marriage, etc.

Homosexuality

(1) God created man to be with woman

(2) It was a capital offense in Old Law

(3) It is strictly condemned in New Law

(4) Homosexuals will not inherit heaven

(5) Homosexuality, like all sin, is a choice

(6) Homosexuality is contrary to the gospel

(7) Homosexuality is not a civil rights issue

(8) Cities were destroyed for homosexuality

(9) Sexual relations are for a man and his wife

(10) Gay marriage is a perversion of God's plan

Footnotes

(1) Genesis 2:24.
(2) Leviticus 20:13.
(3) Romans 1:26-27.
(4) 1 Corinthians 6:9-10.
(5) Romans 1:26-27; 1 Corinthians 6:11.
(6) 1 Timothy 1:10-11.
(7) Homosexuals are not "born that way."
(8) Jude 7.
(9) Matthew 19:4-6; Hebrews 13:4.

Impossibility of Apostasy

(1) "Once saved, always saved"

(2) It was first preached by Satan

(3) It is the fifth tenet of Calvinism

(4) Believers are secure in salvation

(5) Believers can become unbelievers

(6) The apostles could be disqualified

(7) The Hebrew brothers could have fallen

(8) There are several examples of apostasy

(9) "If" statements prove that one can fall away

(10) No one can cause us to lose our salvation

Footnotes

(2) Genesis 3:4.
(3) Perseverance of the Saints (See Calvinism, p.18).
(4) John 5:24.
(5) Hebrews 3:12.
(6) 1 Corinthians 9:27.
(7) Hebrews 3:12-13; 4:1, 11; 10:29, 35; 12:15, 25; 13:9.
(8) Ananias, Sapphira, Hymenaeus, Alexander, Philetus, Demas, etc.
(9) John 8:31; 1 Corinthians 15:2; Galatians 6:9; Colossians 1:23; 2 Peter 1:10.
(10) John 10:27-29.

Can a child of God fall from grace? That question has been discussed and debated many times in various places. It has caused much dissension in the religious world. However, if one will remove all preconceived ideas and denominational prejudices, the answer is clearly revealed in scripture.

According to 1 Timothy, it is possible for a child of God to depart from the faith (4:1), deny the faith (5:8), abandon the faith (5:12), and swerve from the faith (6:21). Surely no one believes that a child of God who does those things is still saved.

The Hebrews were called "holy brothers...who share in a heavenly calling" (3:1). Yet they could fall away from the living God (3:12), be hardened by the deceitfulness of sin (3:13), fail to reach the promise (4:1), fall by the same sort of disobedience (4:11), profane the blood by which they were sanctified (10:29), throw away their confidence (10:35), and be led away by diverse and strange teachings (13:9). Surely no one believes that if the Hebrews did those things they would still be saved.

This is not to say that a child of God has no assurance or confidence, he does. Jesus promised that the believer "does not come into judgment" (John 5:24). However, we must understand that a believer can become an unbeliever. He can develop "an evil, unbelieving heart" (Hebrews 3:12). The blessed assurance of salvation is promised only to those who "continue in the faith" (Colossians 1:23).

There are individuals named in the New Testament who fell away: Ananias and Sapphira (Acts 5:1-11), Hymenaeus and Alexander (1 Timothy 1:19-20), Demas (2 Timothy 4:10), etc. These names are etched in history as a vivid reminder that a child of God can lose his salvation.

Advocates of "once saved, always saved" argue that if an individual falls away, he never really believed in the first place. They say he was only a pretender. However, Jesus made a statement that destroys this argument. In the parable of the sower, He said, "And the ones on the rock are those who, when they hear the word, receive it with joy. But these have no root; they believe for a while, and in time of testing fall away" (Luke 8:13).

Notice that they "believed" and then "fell away." No one can say that they did not really believe, for Jesus said they did! Furthermore, the Israelites are an example of believers who fell away. They "believed in the Lord" (Exodus 14:31) but thousands of them later "fell" (1 Corinthians 10:8). Do not be deceived by such arguments.

Perhaps the most obvious way to prove that a child of God can fall from grace is to look at the word "fall" in scripture. Is it there? If so, how is it used? Here are just some of the passages: "In time of testing fall away" (Luke 8:13); "Take heed lest he fall" (1 Corinthians 10:12); "You have fallen away from grace" (Galatians 5:4); "So that you may not fall under condemnation" (James 5:12); "Remember therefore from where you have fallen" (Revelation 2:5). The fact that the word "fall" is used in reference to Christians settles the issue.

The most graphic description of falling away is found in 2 Peter 2:20-21. Peter wrote, "For if, after they have escaped the defilements of the world through the knowledge of our Lord and Savior Jesus Christ, they are again entangled in them and overcome, the last state is worse for them than the first. For it would have been better for them never to have known the way of righteousness than after knowing it to turn back from the holy commandment delivered to them. What the true proverb says has happened to them: 'The dog returns to its own vomit, and the sow, after washing herself, returns to wallow in the mire.'" Yes, my beloved friends, a child of God can fall from grace!

Indwelling of the Holy Spirit

(1) "Dwell" means to inhabit

(2) Deity dwells in Christians

(3) Deity dwells metaphorically

(4) The Son dwells through faith

(5) The Spirit dwells through faith

(6) The Spirit dwells through Word

(7) The Word is the Spirit's medium

(8) Many things dwell metaphorically

(9) Christians are said to dwell in Deity

(10) Literal indwelling would be miraculous

Footnotes

(2) 1 John 4:12-16; Romans 8:9-11; 1 Corinthians 3:16.

(3) "Dwell" is a figure which denotes close association.

(4) Ephesians 3:17.

(5) Galatians 3:2.

(6) Compare Ephesians 5:18 and Colossians 3:16.

(7) Ephesians 6:17.

(8) Romans 7:17 (sin); Colossians 3:16 (Word); Revelation 2:13 (Satan).

(9) 1 John 4:13-16.

Jehovah's Witnesses

(1) The JW's were founded by Charles T. Russell

(2) The JW's are headquartered in Brooklyn, New York

(3) The JW's have their own translation of the scriptures

(4) The translation changes and perverts the Word of God

(5) The translation committee members were not qualified

(6) The name "Jehovah's Witnesses" was adopted in 1931

(7) The JW's teach that only 144,000 people go to heaven

(8) The JW's teach that Jesus Christ was a created being

(9) The JW's deny the existence of the Holy Spirit

(10) The JW's deny the existence of hell (torment)

Footnotes

(1) Russell: February 16, 1852 (Allegheny, PA) - October 31, 1916 (Pampa, TX).

(3) New World Translation (NWT), published by the Watch Tower Society.

(4) John 1:1 ("a god"); John 8:58 ("I have been"); Colossians 1:16-17 ("other"); etc.

(5) None of the six members had any formal training in biblical languages.

(6) The name is taken from Isaiah 43:10.

(7) This is based on a misunderstanding of the symbolic nature of Revelation 7 and 14.

(8) They say Jesus was created by Jehovah. Jesus is eternal (John 1:1).

(9) They say the Spirit is God's active force. The Spirit is a divine person (Acts 5:3-4).

The Kingdom

(1) "Kingdom" refers to "reign"

(2) The kingdom was prophesied

(3) The kingdom was near in gospels

(4) The kingdom is spiritual in nature

(5) The kingdom is the Lord's church

(6) The kingdom came in the first century

(7) The kingdom will be delivered to God

(8) Jesus never sought an earthly kingdom

(9) The new birth puts one in the kingdom

(10) Premillennialism makes Jesus a failure

Footnotes

(1) It refers to the reign of Christ in the hearts of men.

(2) Daniel 2:44; 7:13-14.

(3) Matthew 3:2; Mark 1:15; 9:1.

(4) Luke 17:20-21.

(5) Matthew 16:18-19; Compare Luke 22:18 and 1 Corinthians 11:17-34.

(6) Colossians 1:13; Hebrews 12:28; Revelation 1:6.

(7) 1 Corinthians 15:24.

(8) John 6:15; 18:36.

(9) John 3:3-5.

(10) It says Jesus intended to set up His kingdom, but did not do so.

The Lord's Death

(1) Jesus was crucified

(2) His death was voluntary

(3) His death was sacrificial

(4) His death was redemptive

(5) His death was prophesied

(6) His death was propitiatory

(7) His death was reconciliatory

(8) His death was foundational

(9) His resurrection was essential

(10) We are baptized into His death

Footnotes
(1) Luke 23:33.
(2) John 10:18.
(3) Hebrews 9:26.
(4) Ephesians 1:7.
(5) 1 Peter 1:10-11.
(6) Romans 3:25.
(7) Romans 5:10.
(8) 1 Corinthians 15:3-4.
(9) 1 Corinthians 15:12-19.
(10) Romans 6:3-5.

The Lord's Supper

(1) It was instituted by the Lord Jesus

(2) It is a memorial of the Lord's death

(3) It is to be eaten in a worthy manner

(4) It is observed on first day of the week

(5) It is observed in the worship assembly

(6) It is a remembrance, not a reenactment

(7) It consists of unleavened bread/fruit of the vine

(8) It looks backward, outward, forward, and inward

(9) It will end when the Lord returns

(10) It is one of five acts of worship

Footnotes

(1) Matthew 26:17-29.

(2) 1 Corinthians 11:23-26.

(3) 1 Corinthians 11:27-29.

(4) Acts 20:7. Christ was raised on first day.

(5) Acts 20:7; 1 Corinthians 11:17-34.

(7) The Lord's Supper was instituted during the Feast of Unleavened Bread.

(8) Backward (remembrance); Outward (proclaim); Forward (until He comes); Inward (examine).

(9) 1 Corinthians 11:26.

(10) The others are singing, praying, preaching, and giving.

On the night He was betrayed, Jesus instituted the Lord's Supper (Matthew 26:17-26; Mark 14:12-15; Luke 22:7-30). This act of worship commemorates and proclaims His death until He comes again (1 Corinthians 11:23-26).

Christians need to observe the Lord's Supper with a sense of reverence. Partakers should meditate upon what they are doing, and why they are doing it. Paul warned that those who eat or drink in an unworthy manner will be guilty of profaning the body and blood of the Lord (1 Corinthians 11:27).

The Lord's Supper consists of unleavened bread and fruit of the vine. We know that the bread is to be unleavened because Jesus instituted the Lord's Supper during the feast of unleavened bread (Matthew 26:17). There would not have been any leaven in the house during that time (Exodus 12:19). The fruit of the vine is unfermented grape juice.

The Lord's Supper is to be observed on the first day of the week (Acts 20:7). The first day of the week is very significant to Christians because it was on the first day that Jesus rose from the dead, the church of Christ was established, and early disciples gathered for worship.

It is striking that Luke, in Acts 20:7, specified the day in which the disciples came together to observe the Lord's Supper. This was not a common feature of his writings. He rarely took time to specify a particular day. However, he wanted his readers to know that this special memorial was reserved for the special day of the week. The Didache, a treatise of early church teachings, says, "But every Lord's day gather yourselves together, and break bread" (14:1) and Justin Martyr wrote that disciples gathered together and observed the Lord's Supper on "the day called Sunday" (Apology 67).

Some argue that since Acts 20:7 does not say "every" first day of the week there is no obligation to observe the Lord's Supper weekly. Such reasoning is illogical. For instance, God commanded the Jews to observe the Sabbath in Exodus 20:8. It says, "Remember the Sabbath day, to keep it holy." Since that verse does not say "every" Sabbath were the Jews at liberty to skip a few? The very thought is absurd. We all recognize that the command to keep holy the Sabbath would include every Sabbath even though it does not use the word "every." The same is true with the Lord's Supper. We are to observe it every Sunday!

If Acts 20:7 said "first day of the year" it would imply a yearly observance. If it said "first day of the month" it would imply a monthly observance. It says "first day of the week" therefore implying a weekly observance!

The Lord's Supper is to be observed in the assembly (Acts 2:42; 20:7). Consider the context of 1 Corinthians 11: "when you come together" (v. 17), "when you come together as a church" (v. 18), "when you come together" (v. 20), "when you come together to eat" (v. 33), "when you come together" (v. 34). Just as the New Testament specifies the day for eating, it also specifies the place of eating. The Lord's Supper is an act of worship that is to observed collectively. If a brother is in a hospital or nursing home and cannot assemble with the saints, he is not required to eat the Lord's Supper.

Mary

(1) She was a native of Nazareth

(2) She was a descendant of David

(3) She was highly favored by God

(4) She had a husband named Joseph

(5) She had a relative named Elizabeth

(6) She conceived Jesus supernaturally

(7) She was at the Lord's crucifixion

(8) She was to be cared for by John

(9) She was in the upper room

(10) She was not ever-virgin

Footnotes

(1) Luke 1:26.

(3) Luke 1:28-30.

(5) Luke 1:36. Elizabeth may have been an aunt since she was much older than Mary.

(6) Matthew 1:18-19.

(7) John 19:25.

(8) John 19:26-27.

(9) Acts 1:14. This is the last mention of Mary. Her last words were in John 2.

(10) Matthew 1:25; 13:55-56.

One does not have to be raised in the Roman Catholic Church (as I was) to know that it puts a great deal of emphasis on Mary. She is called "Mother of God," "Queen of Heaven," "Refuge of Sinners," and much more. There are also special feasts, shrines, and prayers in her honor. In Catholic tradition, few are mentioned more than Mary.

Though Mary was a special maiden who certainly deserves our respect, the Catholic Church has exalted her above measure. She has been given an exaggerated position that goes far beyond scripture. For instance, Catholics pray to Mary, bow before statues of Mary, and see Mary as active in dispensing God's grace. As Monsignor J.D. Conway wrote, "It is the common and explicit teaching of the Church today that every grace given to men comes to them through Mary" (What the Church Teaches, p. 211).

The Catholic view of Mary is perhaps best seen in the highly regarded book *The Glories of Mary*, which bears the Nihil Obstat and the Imprimatur (official declarations that the book has no doctrinal or moral error). Here are some quotes:

P. 17 — "Mary so loved us that she gave her only-begotten son."
(They substituted Mary's name in place of God, John 3:16)

P. 18 — "No one besides Mary has loved us so much as to give an only-begotten and well-beloved Son for us."
(What about God the Father?)

P. 34 — "That pledge is Mary, whom he has given them as a champion or advocate."
(Jesus is our advocate, 1 John 2:1)

P. 44 — "If Mary is for us, who is against us?"
(They substituted Mary's name in place of God, Romans 8:31)

P. 52 — "Mary is the mother and dispenser of every good."
(They substituted Mary's name in place of God, James 1:17)

P. 57 — "She is the city of refuge, the only hope of sinners."
(What about Christ?)

P. 59 — "She restrains her son's hand and withholds him from punishing."
(A mere mortal restraining the hand of God?)

P. 72 — "Mary conquered and bound the devil."
(Jesus destroyed the devil, Hebrews 2:14)

P. 74 — "At the name of Mary every knee bows."
(They substituted Mary's name in place of Jesus, Philippians 2:10)

P. 78 — "Mary's intercession is necessary for salvation."
(Man's salvation depends on a mere mortal?)

P. 87 — "Mary... no one is saved, except through you."
(They substituted Mary in place of Jesus, John 14:6)

P. 95 — "At the command of Mary, everybody obeys, even God."
(blasphemy!)

P. 96 — "Jesus, who is omnipotent, has also made Mary omnipotent."
(They have attributed a divine characteristic to Mary)

Surely one can see that the above quotes are way over the top. They insert Mary's name in place of God and Jesus, attribute to her divine power, and portray her as an essential component of salvation. That is far more than scripture permits.

The last mention of Mary in scripture is in the upper room at Jerusalem (Acts 1:14), which was before the church's establishment. Her name does not appear in the letters of Paul, Peter, James, John, or Jude. This is not said to disparage Mary, but to put our view of her in the proper perspective. She was not the iconic focal point that Catholicism makes her out to be. She faithfully fulfilled her role as the Lord's earthly mother and then faded into the background.

Mary is not honored by creating fanciful traditions that give her positions of power and influence unknown to scripture!

Mormonism

(1) Mormonism was founded by Joseph Smith Jr.

(2) Smith claimed to be visited by an angel (Moroni)

(3) The Book of Mormon was published in 1830

(4) The Book of Mormon contradicts the Bible

(5) The Book of Mormon plagiarizes the Bible

(6) Smith wrote two other books of doctrine

(7) Smith and family had a shady reputation

(8) Smith proved to be a false prophet

(9) Smith was killed by an angry mob

(10) Mormonism is not of God

Footnotes

(1) Smith: December 23, 1805 (Sharon, Vermont) - June 27, 1844 (Carthage, Illinois).

(2) Smith claimed the angel directed him to golden plates on the hill "Cumorah."

(4) Jesus was born in Jerusalem, Christians in B.C. 73, etc.

(5) Compare 1 Corinthians 13:4-8 (KJV) with Moroni 7:45-46.

(6) "Doctrine and Covenants" and "Pearl of Great Price."

(7) 62 residents of Palmyra, NY signed statement to that effect. Smith was later accused of fraud, violence, treason, etc.

(8) Deuteronomy 18:22. (Smith prophesied that a temple would be built in Independence, MO in his generation).

(10) Galatians 1:6-9.

Music of the Church

(1) The early church sang in worship

(2) There were no special singing groups

(3) There were no mechanical instruments

(4) They sang psalms, hymns, and spiritual songs

(5) "Psallo" in Ephesians 5:19 means to sing praise

(6) Religious leaders condemned using instruments

(7) Singing and playing are distinct acts of worship

(8) "A cappella" means "in manner of the church"

(9) The Christian's instrument is the human heart

(10) Singing is one of five acts of worship

Footnotes

(1) 1 Corinthians 14:15.

(2) The singing was congregational (Ephesians 5:19).

(3) Mechanical instruments were not introduced until 7th century.

(4) Ephesians 5:19; Colossians 3:16.

(5) Respected lexicographers agree on this definition (Thayer, Mounce, Arndt-Gingrich, etc).

(6) Martin Luther, John Calvin, John Wesley, Charles Spurgeon, etc.

(7) 2 Chronicles 29:28.

(8) "A cappella" is singing without musical accompaniment.

(10) The others are praying, preaching, Lord's Supper, and giving.

There can be no denying that the early church sang in worship to God (1 Corinthians 14:15; Hebrews 2:12). That is not the issue. The issue is whether or not it is appropriate to add mechanical instruments to the singing. It may surprise some to know that in New Testament times, singing was never accompanied by the use of mechanical instruments. In other words, their music was a cappella. They sang, but never played!

Notable Quotes

Although the following quotes are not our authority, they do illustrate the fact that mechanical instruments were not part of the divine pattern and faced strong opposition since they were introduced.

John Calvin: "Musical instruments in celebrating the praises of God would be no more suitable than the burning of incense, the lighting up of lamps, and the restoration of the other shadows of the law. The Papists, therefore, have foolishly borrowed this, as well as many other things, from the Jews."

Charles Spurgeon: "What a degradation to supplant the intelligent song of the whole congregation by the theatrical prettinesses of a quartette, the refined niceties of a choir, or the blowing off of wind from inanimate bellows and pipes! We might as well pray by machinery as praise by it."

John Wesley: "I have no objection to instruments of music in our chapels provided they are neither HEARD nor SEEN."

David Benedict (Baptist historian): "Staunch old Baptists in former times would as soon have tolerated the Pope of Rome in their pulpits as an organ in their galleries."

The Catholic Encyclopedia: "Although Josephus tells of the wonderful effects produced in the Temple by the use of instruments, the first Christians were of too spiritual a fibre to substitute lifeless instruments for or to use them to accompany the human voice. Clement of Alexandria severely condemns the use of instruments even at Christian banquets."

Answering Arguments

(1) *There will be instruments in heaven.* If one could prove that there will be instruments in heaven, they still have not found authority for their use in the worship of the church. There are many things in heaven that are not in the church (infants, angels, etc.), and there are many things in the church that will not be in heaven (marriage, Lord's Supper, etc). Those who make this argument usually refer to passages in the book of Revelation, which forewarns that it was written in figurative language (1:1, "signified," KJV). Does anyone really believe that spirit beings will play material instruments?

(2) *Instruments are an aid.* An "aid" helps in fulfilling a command without changing the very nature of the command. An "addition" changes the very nature of the command. Noah was commanded to build an ark of gopher wood (Genesis 6:14). In building the ark, he used certain tools such as a hammer and saw. Were those tools aids or additions? Since they helped in fulfilling the command to build an ark of gopher wood without changing the very nature of the command, they would classify as aids. However, if Noah had used pine or oak in constructing the ark, he would have changed the very nature of the command. Hence, those things would classify as additions. Now compare that to mechanical instruments. Do they help in fulfilling the command to sing or are they an addition to the singing? Clearly they are an addition. No longer is one simply singing. He is now playing!

(3) *David used instruments in worship.* Our authority must come from the New Testament. The Old Testament is not our standard. David is not our standard. However, let us take this argument to its logical conclusion. If David using instruments authorizes us to do so, then we can also have multiple wives and kill our enemies. If not, why not? David did! Furthermore, David kept the Sabbath and offered animal sacrifices. Does that mean we should too? To ask the question is to answer it.

(4) *The word "psallo" (making melody) means to pluck an instrument.* If that is so, then every member must pluck an instrument. Yet I know of no one who takes such a position. We must understand that words evolve over time. By the first century, the word *"psallo"* simply meant to sing praise (see Liddell-Scott; Thayer; Mounce; Arndt-Gingrich, etc).

While there are other arguments that some make to defend the use of mechanical instruments, these four are the ones that probably rate the highest in use and strength. Even they, however, will not survive the scrutiny of examination. Musical instruments in worship are indefensible!

One Cup Controversy

(1) Some oppose multiple cups in communion

(2) They argue that only one cup was used by Jesus

(3) They argue that multiple cups were a late addition

(4) They argue that the cup (container) represents NT

(5) Christians in different places drank of same cup

(6) "Cup" comes from the Greek word *"poterion"*

(7) "Cup" is used by metonymy for its contents

(8) "Cup" represents the Lord's blood

(9) Multiple cups are authorized

(10) It is sinful to make laws

Footnotes

(1) Opponents of multiple containers are often called "One Cup" advocates.

(2) This is a mere assumption. The Passover Feast provided for each person to have his own cup.

(3) The NT is silent on this point. It is hard to imagine 5,000 using same container (Acts 4:4).

(4) There are only two elements of the Lord's Supper (1 Corinthains 10:16), not three.

(5) 1 Corinthians 10:16.

(6) *"Poterion"* can refer to the vessel or to the contents within the vessel.

(7) "Metonymy" is a figure of speech in which the name of one thing is put forth for another associated with it.

(8) Jesus said the cup was His blood (Matthew 26:28). It could be drunk, divided, etc.

(9) Cups aid in fulfilling command ("drink") without changing nature of command (general authority).

(10) Man has no right binding where God has not bound.

Paul

(1) His Hebrew name was Saul

(2) He was a Roman citizen by birth

(3) He was a native of Tarsus in Cilicia

(4) He was a student of the rabbi Gamaliel

(5) He was a persecutor of the church

(6) He was an apostle to the Gentiles

(7) He was the writer of 13 epistles

(8) He was a tentmaker by trade

(9) He was prominent in Acts

(10) He was martyred

Footnotes

(1) Acts 13:9.

(2) Acts 22:25-29. Roman citizenship was either inherited or purchased.

(3) Acts 22:3.

(4) Acts 22:3. Gamaliel was a teacher of the Law (Acts 5:34).

(5) Galatians 1:13.

(6) Romans 11:13.

(7) It is doubtful that Paul wrote Hebrews (see 2 Thessalonians 3:17; Hebrews 2:3).

(8) Acts 18:3. It was customary for Jewish fathers to teach their sons a trade.

(9) Acts 13-28.

(10) Tradition says that he was beheaded by Nero.

Peter & The Papacy

(1) "Pope" comes from the Latin word "papa"

(2) Catholics say the Pope is the Vicar of Christ

(3) The office of Pope is never mentioned in NT

(4) There is no evidence that Peter lived in Rome

(5) Peter never claimed primacy over the apostles

(6) Jesus said that no one is greater in the kingdom

(7) James had final say in the Jerusalem meeting

(8) Peter and John were sent by other apostles

(9) Boniface III was the first to assume title

(10) Peter never called himself "Pope"

Footnotes

(1) "Papa" means "father." Jesus said "call no man your father" in a religious sense (Matthew 23:9).

(2) "Vicar" means "one who presides in place of another." Jesus is the sole "Chief Shepherd" (1 Peter 5:4).

(3) Ephesians 4:11 mentions several offices in the early church, but not the Pope.

(5) Peter was rebuked publicly by Paul (Galatians 2:11-14).

(6) Luke 22:24-30.

(7) Acts 15:13-21.

(8) Acts 8:14.

(9) Gregory I refused title ("Universal Bishop") in A.D. 604. Boniface III accepted it in A.D. 607.

(10) Peter identified himself as a servant, apostle, elder, etc., but never Pope.

Plagues on Egypt

(1) There were 10 plagues on Egypt

(2) The plagues are recorded in Exodus

(3) The plagues assaulted Egyptian gods

(4) The plagues followed a threefold pattern

(5) The plagues steadily intensified in severity

(6) The plagues can be divided into five groups

(7) The Hebrews were exempt from seven plagues

(8) Pharaoh released Hebrews after the tenth plague

(9) The plagues are summarized in the Psalms

(10) The plagues manifested divine power

Footnotes

(1) Water to blood, frogs, gnats, flies, livestock death, boils, hail, locusts, darkness, firstborn death.

(2) Exodus 7-12.

(3) Exodus 12:12.

(4) Outdoor morning confrontation (1, 4, 7); indoor court confrontation (2, 5, 8); no confrontation (3, 6, 9).

(6) River (1, 2), nuisance (3, 4), disease (5, 6), destruction (7, 8), darkness (9, 10).

(8) Exodus 12:31-32.

(9) Psalm 78:44-51; 105:28-36.

(10) They were predicted, progressive, partial, etc.

Religious Titles

(1) Religious titles are not to be worn

(2) Religious titles were not worn by early church

(3) Religious titles promote clergy/laity distinction

(4) Scriptural designations are not to be worn as titles

(5) "Reverend" in Psalm 111:9 refers to God's name

(6) "Father" is not to be worn as religious title

(7) "Pastor" is not to be worn as religious title

(8) The humble will not wear religious titles

(9) We are simply to be called "brothers"

(10) Early Baptists rejected "Reverend"

Footnotes
(1) Matthew 23:8-12.
(2) NT preachers never wore titles. We do not read of "Reverend Paul" or "Cardinal John."
(3) Every member is equal. There should be no special titles, seat, robes, etc.
(4) "Bishop," "Elder," "Pastor," etc. are scriptural terms, but were never worn as titles.
(5) KJV. The Psalmist was referring to God's name.
(6) Matthew 23:9. "Father" can be used in a secular sense (Acts 16:1).
(7) "Pastor" is found in Ephesians 4:11, KJV.
(8) How can a man be "poor in spirit" (Matthew 5:3) while exalting himself with titles?
(9) Matthew 23:8; 1 Corinthians 16:12; Hebrews 13:23.
(10) See "50 Years Among the Baptists," David Benedict, p. 286.

The wearing of religious titles has long been commonplace in Christendom. It is a practice that most people accept without much consideration, just assuming that it is okay. In fact, they are surprised when preachers do not wear such titles.

One would be hard pressed to list all of the religious titles in existence. Reverend, Bishop, Archbishop, Father, Your Holiness, Your Eminence, Doctor, Pastor, and Elder are just a few examples. There are even titles for the preacher's wife (like "First Lady") and web pages that provide instruction on "clergy etiquette." Below are two excerpts.

Greeting Clergy in Person

When we address Deacons or Priests, we should use the title "Father." Bishops we should address as "Your Grace." Though all Bishops (including Patriarchs) are equal in the Orthodox Church, they do have different administrative duties and honors that accrue to their rank in this sense. Thus, "Your Eminence" is the proper title for Bishops with suffragans or assistant Bishops, Metropolitans, and most Archbishops (among the exceptions to this rule is the Archbishop of Athens, who is addressed as "Your Beatitude"). "Your Beatitude" is the proper title for Patriarchs (except for the Ecumenical Patriarch in Constantinople, who is addressed as "Your All--Holiness"). When we approach an Orthodox Presbyter or Bishop (but not a Deacon), we make a bow by reaching down and touching the floor with our right hand, place our right hand over the left (palms upward), and say: "Bless, Father" (or "Bless, Your Grace," or "Bless, Your Eminence," etc.). The Priest or Bishop then answers, "May the Lord bless you," blesses us with the Sign of the Cross, and places his right hand in our hands. We kiss then his hand.

Addressing Clergy in a Letter

When we write to a clergyman (and, by custom, monastics), we should open our letter with the greeting, "Bless, Father." At the end of the letter, it is customary to close with the following line: "Kissing your right hand…" It is not appropriate to invoke a blessing on a clergyman, as many do: "May God bless you." Not only does this show a certain spiritual arrogance before the image of the cleric, but laymen do not have the Grace of the Priesthood and the prerogative to bless in their stead. (Orthodox Christian Information Center, Clergy Etiquette, orthodoxinfo.com).

Though the wearing of religious titles is a prevalent practice, it should be judged by the same standard that all other things are judged. Where is the scriptural authority?

Why Titles Are Wrong

(1) *They are specifically condemned.* In Matthew 23, Jesus mentioned the special dress, special seats, and special titles of the scribes and Pharisees. Then He said, "But you are not to be called rabbi, for you have one teacher, and you are all brothers. And call no man your father on earth, for you have one Father, who is in heaven. Neither be called instructors, for you have one instructor, the Christ" (vv. 8-10). Notice that Jesus did not want His disciples to wear titles like the religious leaders of the day.

(2) *They were not worn in the early church.* The first Christians did not use religious titles. Not even the most respected preachers wore them. For instance, Apollos (1 Corinthians 16:12), Timothy (Hebrews 13:23), and Paul (2 Peter 3:15) were simply called "brother."

(3) *They exalt some above others.* Disciples are not to elevate themselves above one another. Rather, they are to maintain a servant's spirit (Matthew 18:1-4; 20:25-28; 23:11-12). By their very nature, religious titles exalt some above others.

(4) *They reflect a clergy/laity distinction.* There is no such thing as a clergy/laity distinction in the New Testament. However, when men assume titles that elevate them above other members (or wear special clothing, sit in special seats, etc), such a distinction can hardly be avoided.

These are just a few obvious reasons why men should not wear religious titles. They have no place in the church of our Lord Jesus.

Reverend

The term "reverend" appears one time in the King James Version (KJV). Psalm 111:9 says, "He sent redemption unto his people: he hath commanded his covenant for ever: holy and reverend is his name." Notice that "reverend" is used in that passage of God. It is the height of presumption for men to take a term used only in reference to God and apply it to themselves!

Below are two quotes from Baptist sources condemning the practice of calling men "Reverend." This is especially noteworthy considering so many Baptist preachers are addressed by that title.

> Some of the words used by the Baptists of today in their preaching, writing, and conversation are altogether alien to the verbiage of the early Christians. Who could imagine Onesimus going to Philemon and talking to him about "The Reverend Paul?" Who could imagine Gaius writing to the "Reverend John" to give him a good report about the "Reverend Demetrius?" Yet modern Baptists use the term "Reverend" every day in speaking of preachers or writing about them... If the Baptists of the medieval age could hear it today they would cry against the use of this title which has been borrowed from an ecclesiastical hierarchy that would draw a line between the laity and the ministry. When the word "Reverend" is used in the Bible, it refers to God, for He alone is to be revered. (Baptist Standard, Editorial Section, April 9, 1955, p. 2).

The term Reverend, now in such common use among our people and all other parties, was generally very offensive to Baptists of the old school, and was seldom employed by them in common conversation, in letter inscriptions, or in any other way. Holy and reverend is his name, as a designation of the Divine Being, was a passage often quoted by objectors to giving reverence to men. To the Deity alone, said they, reverence belongs. (50 Years Among the Baptists, David Benedict, p. 286).

Scriptural Terms

The fact that some of the titles worn by men are scriptural terms (like "elder" or "pastor") does not justify the practice under discussion because they were never worn as titles in the early church. They were used as designations. For instance, Peter referred to himself as simply "a fellow elder" (1 Peter 5:1), not as "Elder Peter."

Conclusion

Let us refrain from using religious titles. They are not pleasing to the Lord; they are foreign to the New Testament; they exalt some above others; and they produce pride.

The Sabbath

(1) "Sabbath" means "rest"

(2) It was first mentioned in Exodus 16

(3) It was first instituted at Mount Sinai

(4) It was a memorial of Egyptian slavery

(5) It was given specifically to Israelites

(6) It was nailed to the cross of Christ

(7) It was never commanded in NT

(8) We observe first day of week

(9) 10 Commandments obsolete

(10) No one truly keeps Sabbath

Footnotes

(2) Exodus 16:23.

(3) Nehemiah 9:13-14. There was no mention of anyone keeping the Sabbath before Moses.

(4) Deuteronomy 5:15.

(5) Exodus 31:12-17. Hosea 2:11 speaks of "her" Sabbaths, referring to Israel.

(6) Colossians 2:14-16.

(7) Ignatius, Irenaeus, Eusebius, etc. all taught that the Sabbath was abolished.

(8) Acts 20:7; 1 Corinthians 16:2. Jesus was raised from the dead on the first day of the week.

(9) 2 Corinthians 3:6-14.

(10) Sabbath keeping included no work, no travel, burnt offerings, execution of violators, etc.

Satan

(1) "Satan" means "adversary"

(2) Satan is the leader of fallen angels

(3) Satan is an actual personality of evil

(4) Satan's evil character is seen in OT

(5) Satan's evil character is seen in NT

(6) Satan is referred to in many ways

(7) Satan is the accuser of God/man

(8) Satan will be condemned to hell

(9) Satan fell because of pride

(10) Satan is not "Lucifer"

Footnotes

(1) "Satan" is the personal name of the devil (Matthew 4:10).

(2) Matthew 25:41; Revelation 12:7.

(3) He speaks, lies, blinds, tempts, devours, contends, etc.

(4) He tempted Eve, attacked Job, incited David, accused Joshua the high priest, etc.

(5) He tempted Jesus, entered Judas, blinded unbelievers, hindered Paul, etc.

(6) He is called devil, enemy, father of lies, ruler of this world, tempter, evil one, etc.

(7) He accuses God to man (Genesis 3:4) and man to God (Job 1:9; 2:4).

(8) Matthew 25:41; Revelation 20:10.

(9) 1 Timothy 3:6.

(10) "Lucifer" in Isaiah 14:12 (KJV) refers to the king of Babylon.

Satan is a spirit being who opposes God and man. He "prowls around like a roaring lion, seeking someone to devour" (1 Peter 5:8). From the first book of the Old Testament to the last book of the New Testament, we read about the existence of a personality of evil called Satan.

Satan is the personal name of the diabolical ruler of evil spirits. He is referred to in scripture in many ways, including "the devil" (1 John 3:8), "the tempter" (1 Thessalonians 3:5), "the evil one" (1 John 3:12), "the god of this world" (2 Corinthians 4:4), "the ruler of this world" (John 12:31), "the prince of demons" (Matthew 9:34), "the prince of the power of the air" (Ephesians 2:2), "the father of lies" (John 8:44), "the enemy" (Matthew 13:39), "the dragon" (Revelation 12:7), "the accuser" (Revelation 12:10), "the serpent" (2 Corinthians 11:3), "Belial" (2 Corinthians 6:15), and "Apollyon" (Revelation 9:11). One name not mentioned in the list is "Lucifer." That is because Satan is never called Lucifer in the Bible. The reference to Lucifer in Isaiah 14:12 (KJV) refers to the king of Babylon, not to Satan.

Satan appears in scripture as an actual personality of evil. He speaks (Matthew 4:3), tempts (1 Corinthians 7:5), deceives (Revelation 12:9), challenges (Job 1:11), accuses (Revelation 12:10), lies (John 8:44), contends (Jude 9), incites (1 Chronicles 21:1), murders (John 8:44), hinders (1 Thessalonians 2:18), flees (James 4:7), devours (1 Peter 5:8), blinds (2 Corinthians 4:4), and sins (1 John 3:8). He possesses intelligence and purpose (Genesis 3:1-6).

Satan was probably created before the foundation of the earth with all the angels of heaven (Job 38:4-7). He was not created evil, but chose to rebel against God. This is not hard to imagine when we consider that the New Testament mentions angels who "sinned" (2 Peter 2:4) and "did not stay within their own position of authority, but left their proper dwelling" (Jude 6). Since the scriptures refer to Satan as "the prince of demons" (Matthew 9:34; 12:24) and speak of fallen angels as "his angels" (Matthew 25:41; Revelation 12:7), it is probably safe to conclude that he is the leader of the fallen angels. Further, he is considered the author of sin (1 John 3:8), sickness (Acts 10:38), and death (Hebrews 2:14). He is credited with leading men astray (2 Thessalonians 2:9-10). He is our foe!

Satan is powerful, but not all-powerful. He is limited in what he can do. We see that clearly in the testing of Job. Satan had to get permission to test Job, and was able to inflict suffering upon Job only to the extent that God permitted (Job 1:12; 2:6). While tempting Jesus, Satan stated that the kingdoms of the world were "delivered" to him (Luke 4:6), which indicates he did not acquire them by his own power. The church at Smyrna was assured that their tribulation would be short — "ten days" (Revelation 2:10). In order for Satan to succeed, we must "give... opportunity" to him (Ephesians 4:27). Perhaps nothing demonstrates this point more than the fate awaiting him. Satan will be unable to resist being thrown into hell on the great Day of Judgment. Finally, Satan could not stop Jesus from being born, induce Him to sin, or keep Him in the tomb.

• Satan uses weaknesses to entice us (1 Corinthians 7:5)
• Satan employs the allurements of the world (1 John 2:15-17)
• Satan induces men to believe a lie (2 Thessalonians 2:9-10)
• Satan is ferocious in his attacks (1 Peter 5:8)
• False religion is Satan's religion—he has a synagogue (Revelation 2:9)
• Satan changes the Word (Genesis 3:4)
• Satan misapplies the Word (Matthew 4:6-7)
• Satan was created (Colossians 1:16)
• Satan uses men who appear righteous to teach error (2 Corinthians 11:13-15)
• Satan accuses God to man (Genesis 3:6) and man to God (Job 1:9; 2:4)
• Satan can be resisted (James 4:7; 1 Peter 5:9)

The belief that Satan does not exist may be one of his greatest achievements. People will not guard against somebody they do not believe can hurt them. Others may claim to believe in the existence of a personality of evil called Satan, but their actions indicate that they do not fear him. For instance, would someone joke about Satan or dress up as Satan if they really considered him a threat to their soul? Do you suppose that Jesus or the apostles would find pleasure in someone parading around with horns and a tail claiming to be "the devil?" Satan's genius is on display when humans engage in such behavior.

The Second Coming

(1) There will be a Second Coming

(2) The Lord will come from heaven

(3) The Lord will appear in the clouds

(4) His return will be audible/visible

(5) His return will be unannounced

(6) His return will be with angels

(7) There will be a resurrection

(8) The earth will be destroyed

(9) Judgment will take place

(10) We are to be waiting

Footnotes

(1) Hebrews 9:28.
(2) Acts 1:11.
(3) 1 Thessalonians 4:17.
(4) 1 Corinthians 15:52 (audible); Revelation 1:7 (visible).
(5) Matthew 24:42-44.
(6) 2 Thessalonians 1:7.
(7) 1 Thessalonians 4:16.
(8) 2 Peter 3:10-12.
(9) Matthew 25:31-33.
(10) Titus 2:13.

The Seven Letters

(1) The letters are in Revelation 2-3

(2) The letters were penned by John

(3) The letters were authored by Jesus

(4) The letters addressed actual problems

(5) The letters were sent to congregations

(6) The letters are representative in nature

(7) The letters follow a sevenfold pattern

(8) Two letters contain no condemnation

(9) One letter contains no commendation

(10) Each congregation was autonomous

Footnotes

(2) John was on a small island called "Patmos" (Revelation 1:9).

(5) They were in Ephesus, Smyrna, Pergamum, Thyatira, Sardis, Philadelphia, and Laodicea.

(6) Though sent to actual congregations, they have a universal application.

(7) Commission, character, commendation, condemnation, correction, call, and challenge.

(8) Smyrna and Philadelphia.

(9) Laodicea.

The Social Gospel

(1) The church has a threefold work

(2) The social gospel is another gospel

(3) The social gospel markets the church

(4) The social gospel perverts Christ's mission

(5) The social gospel depreciates gospel's power

(6) The social gospel leaves man spiritually starving

(7) The mission of the church is spiritual in nature

(8) The early church never used games and gimmicks

(9) Entertainment and recreation is a work of the home

(10) We are to eat our common meals at home

Footnotes

(1) Benevolence, edification, and evangelism (BEE).

(2) Galatians 1:6. The social gospel appeals to man with fun, food, and frolic.

(3) Whatever man "needs" is replaced by whatever man "wants."

(4) Luke 19:10. Christ came to save, not to entertain.

(5) Romans 1:16. The gospel does not need basketball goals to score conversions.

(8) Sports were prevalent in first century (1 Corinthians 9:24-27), but never used by church.

(10) 1 Corinthians 11:22, 34.

The Ten Commandments

(1) They are called "Decalogue"

(2) They are recorded two times

(3) They were part of the Old Law

(4) They were given at Mount Sinai

(5) They were given to the Israelites

(6) The first four commands are vertical

(7) The last six commands are horizontal

(8) Nine of the commands are found in NT

(9) They were spoken directly to the people

(10) They are moral absolutes

Footnotes

(1) Decalogue: *"deka"* (ten) and *"logos"* (word).
(2) Exodus 20:1-17; Deuteronomy 5:1-21.
(3) Romans 7:7.
(6) Our duty to God (vertical).
(7) Our duty to man (horizontal).
(8) Sabbath observance is not commanded in NT. ("First day" -- Acts 20:7; 1 Corinthians 16:2).
(10) "You shall" and "You shall not."

Tithing

(1) "Tithe" means "tenth"

(2) Some patriarchs tithed

(3) Tithing was part of Old Law

(4) Tithing improperly was robbery

(5) Tithing was not peculiar to Israel

(6) Tithing was not commanded in NT

(7) Tithing was not mentioned by Paul

(8) Tithing was not bound on Gentiles

(9) Christians gave as they prospered

(10) We should not bind Old Law

Footnotes

(2) Genesis 14:20; 28:22. It was voluntary.

(3) Leviticus 27:30.

(4) Malachi 3:8-12.

(7) This writer does not believe that Paul wrote Hebrews.

(8) Acts 15:28-29.

(9) 1 Corinthians 16:1-2. New Testament giving is based on prosperity, not percentage.

(10) The same principle that condemned binding circumcision applies to tithing.

Tongue Speaking

(1) Tongues were a spiritual gift

(2) Tongues were known languages

(3) Tongues were regulated in assembly

(4) Tongues were confirmatory in nature

(5) Tongues were not necessary for salvation

(6) Tongues are mentioned in three NT books

(7) All spiritual gifts ceased when NT completed

(8) Early writers considered tongues obsolete

(9) Tongue speakers maintained self-control

(10) No one today has the gift of tongues

Footnotes

(1) 1 Corinthians 12:8-10.
(2) Acts 2:4-8.
(3) 1 Corinthians 14:27-35.
(4) 1 Corinthians 14:22.
(5) 1 Corinthians 12:30.
(6) Mark, Acts, and 1 Corinthians.
(7) 1 Corinthians 13:8-10. NRSV says "complete."
(8) Chrysostom, Augustine, etc.
(9) 1 Corinthians 14:32. It was not an uncontrolled frenzy.

Work Ethic

(1) God demands strong work ethic

(2) Work commanded before the fall

(3) Work commanded in the Decalogue

(4) God and Jesus had strong work ethic

(5) The apostles had strong work ethic

(6) The Jews had strong work ethic

(7) Laziness is condemned by God

(8) Proverbs rebukes the sluggard

(9) Christians are to be providers

(10) Work must be prioritized

Footnotes

(1) Ephesians 4:28; Colossians 3:22-24; 1 Thessalonians 4:11.

(2) Genesis 2:15.

(3) Exodus 20:9.

(4) Genesis 2:2; Mark 6:3.

(5) Acts 20:34-35; 1 Thessalonians 2:9; 2 Thessalonians 3:7-8.

(6) Jewish Saying: "He who does not teach his son a trade, teaches him to steal."

(7) 2 Thessalonians 3:10.

(8) Proverbs 6:6-9; 10:26; 13:4; 15:19; 19:24; 20:4; 21:25; 22:13; 24:30; 26:13-16.

(9) Acts 20:35; Ephesians 4:28; 1 Timothy 5:8.

(10) We must not put work before worship or family.

Worship

(1) Worship is homage to God

(2) Not all worship is acceptable

(3) There is a pattern for worship in NT

(4) Worship must be in spirit and in truth

(5) Unauthorized worship is serious offense

(6) Worship is not to entertain the worshipper

(7) Worship must be done decently and in order

(8) There are many perversions in worship today

(9) We are to worship God with reverence and awe

(10) God alone is to be worshipped

Footnotes

(1) Worship is a distinct act in scripture (Genesis 22:5; 2 Samuel 12:20; Acts 8:27).

(2) Hebrews 12:28 speaks of "acceptable worship," which implies that some worship is unacceptable.

(3) The pattern includes singing, praying, preaching, giving, and eating the Lord's Supper.

(4) John 4:24.

(5) Leviticus 10:1-2.

(6) Worship is to please God, not ourselves. He is the focal point.

(7) 1 Corinthians 14:40. Sensationalism and spontaneity do not equate with spirituality.

(8) Monthly observances of the Lord's Supper, special singing groups, women preachers, instruments, etc.

(9) Hebrews 12:28. Punctuality, enthusiasm, clothing, etc. are all good indicators of how seriously we view worship.

(10) Matthew 4:10. We are not to worship men, angels, images, nature, etc. We are to "worship God" (Revelation 22:9).